# FOREVER
## FIFTY
### AND OTHER
### NEGOTIATIONS

# FOREVER FIFTY

# AND OTHER NEGOTIATIONS

## Judith Viorst

Thorndike Press • Thorndike, Maine

**Library of Congress Cataloging in Publication Data:**

Viorst, Judith.
    Forever fifty and other negotiations / Judith Viorst.
    p.  cm.
    ISBN 0-89621-989-5 (lg. print : alk. paper)
    1. Middle age--Poetry. 2. Aging--Poetry. 3. Large type
    books. I. Title.
[PS3572.I6F6    1990]               90-10796
811'.54--dc20                       CIP

Thorndike Press Large Print edition published in 1990
by arrangement with Simon & Schuster, Inc.

Cover design by John Alcorn.

**The trees indicium is a trade mark of Thorndike
Press.**

This book is printed on acid-free, high opacity paper. ∞

again, for Milton

# FOREVER FIFTY

# AND OTHER NEGOTIATIONS
# BY JUDITH VIORST

# CONTENTS

## FOREVER FIFTY

# FIFTY

# YOU SAY YOU WANT TO KNOW HOW OLD I AM?

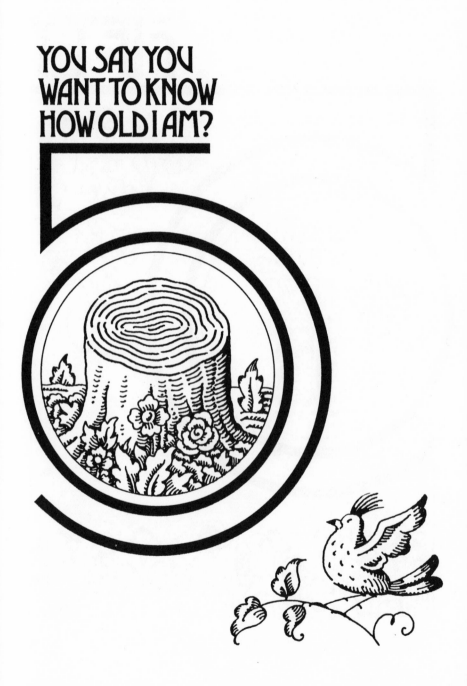

I don't mind telling my age. I
    honestly don't mind telling my age.
But why are you asking?

I don't pretend I'm still young. I
    don't expect to be thought of as
        young.
So why are you asking?

I never lie about age. It's
    undignified to lie about age.
But why are you asking?

We're only as old as we feel. You
    know we're only as old as we feel.
So why are you asking?

I'm told I look good for my age. I'm
        often told I look good for my age.
Now why are you asking?

No, I'm not ashamed of my age. And
        if you insist, I'll tell you my age.
You're what? Still asking?

YOU SAY YOU WANT
TO KNOW HOW THE
CHILDREN ARE DOING?

# YOU SAY YOU WANT TO KNOW HOW THE CHILDREN ARE DOING?

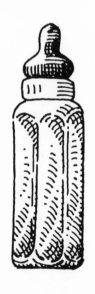

Shawn teaches wind-surfing. Dawn is a
   certified midwife.
Kim has converted from atheist to
   Bahai.
Justin has finally fallen in love with a
   practically
      perfect person,
Except he's a guy.

Holly quit teaching first grade to go
   into arbitrage.
Keith runs a health club and Kyle's a
   computer whiz.
Robin, who's on her second divorce
   and fourth therapist, feels
      that she's starting
To learn who she is.

Brandon has dropped out of medical
    school to write screenplays.
Josh has abjured material wealth to do
    good.
Kirsten and Stacy and Maya and Tracy
    have opted for
        partnership track
Over motherhood.

Andrea is a professional acupuncturist.
Damian's making a killing in real estate.
Tara has already given birth to Rebecca
    and Joseph and Jacob,
And plans to have eight.

Kevin has given up socks and acquired
    two earrings.
Devon has given up sweets and eats
    nothing impure.
And so, if you want to know how the
    children are doing,
The answer is,
We're not exactly sure.

# WILD THING

# WILD THING

I went for a walk in the sun without
  wearing my sunscreen.
I went out of town without making a
  reservation.
I placed my mouth directly upon a
  public drinking fountain,
    and took a sip.
I didn't bother flossing my teeth before
  bedtime.
I pumped my own gasoline at a
  self-service station.
I ate the deviled egg instead of the
  cauliflower with low-fat
    yoghurt dip.
I bought, without reading *Consumer
  Reports*, a new dryer.

I left my checking account
  unreconciled.
I know that the consequences could be
  dire,
But sometimes a woman simply has to
  run wild.

# EXERCISING OPTIONS

# EXERCISING OPTIONS

I've been told that the vigorous
     moving-about of my body
Could discourage all ills from loose
     flesh to a heart attack.
But there isn't a fitness routine
That strikes me as anything less than
     obscene, so
I float on my back.

I respect those brave ladies who're
     burning their flab off
          with Fonda.
They still wear bikinis. I long ago
     switched to a sack.
But my horror of thickening thighs
Is surpassed by my horror of exercise, so
I float on my back.

I admire all those stalwarts out jogging
in blizzards and heat
waves
But if I want torture, I'd just as soon
head for the rack.
Let my upper arms droop, I aspire
To no exertion that makes me perspire,
so
I float on my back.

And I know that I richly deserve the
whole world's condemnation
For the firmness that both my torso
and character lack.
Yes, my body's a total disgrace
But there is this big happy smile on my
face as
I float on my back.

# POSTMORTEMS

# POSTMORTEMS

On the way home with my husband
     from the dinner party,
I thought I'd very tactfully point out
That he shouldn't interrupt, and that
He shouldn't talk with his hands, and
     that
He shouldn't, when discussing politics,
     shout.
And that he shouldn't tell that story
     while people
          are eating, and that
He shouldn't tell that joke for the rest
     of his
          life, and that
He shouldn't have said what he said
     about that
          terrible lady in red because

She happens to be
   the-person-he-said-it-to's wife.
And that he didn't need that second
   helping of
       mousse cake, and that
He didn't need to finish the
   Chardonnay.
But after thirty years of marriage
I finally understand what not to say
On the way home with my husband
   from a
       dinner party.

# CONFUSION

# CONFUSION

I can't figure out if it's gas or a coronary.
I can't figure out if it's hostile or benign.
I can't figure out if I'm turning into a
     hypochondriac,
          or just being sensible.
I can't figure out when we stop
     supporting our children.
(At twenty-one? At thirty? Forty-nine?)
I can't figure out if not bothering to
     change the sheets in the
          guest room in between houseguests
               is ever an option, or
          always reprehensible.

I can't figure out why men won't ask
     for directions.
(Is this genetic or could they be
     retrained?)

I can't figure out, when dressed in the
    height of fashion, if
        I'm looking incredibly chic or
            slightly ridiculous.
I can't figure out if my tale is enthralling
    or boring.
(What are those facial expressions?
    Spellbound? Or pained?)
I can't figure out if wanting all the
    hangers in my closet to
        face the same way means I'm
            obsessive-compulsive, or
            merely meticulous.

I can't figure out if I've gone from stable
    to stodgy.
(Is "reliable" what I want as my
    epitaph?)
I can't figure out if helping yourself to
    a shrimp from your
        spouse's plate ought to be viewed
            as intimacy or intrusion.
I can't figure out if I've lost my sense of
    humor

Or if, after fifty, it just gets harder to
  laugh.
And I can't figure out if everyone else
  has figured everything
    out, or whether we are all in a state
    of confusion.

# TO A MIDDLE~AGED FRIEND CONSIDERING ADULTERY WITH A YOUNGER MAN

It's hard to be devil-may-care
When there are pleats in your derrière
And it's time to expose what your panty
    hose
        are concealing.
And although a husband's fond eyes
Make certain allowances for your thighs,
Young lovers might look less benignly
    at what
        you're revealing.

It's hard to surrender to sin
While trying to hold your stomach in
And hoping your blusher's still
    brightening up
        your complexion,

And hoping he isn't aware
As he runs his fingers through your
    dark hair,
That you've grown unmistakably gray
    in a whole
        other section.

It's hard to experience bliss
When sinus intrudes on every kiss
And when, in the tricky positions, your
    back
        starts to hurt you.
And when you add all it entails
To teach him what turns you on and
    what fails,
You might want to reconsider the
    virtues of
        virtue.

# HAPPINESS

# HAPPINESS

# (RECONSIDERED)

Happiness
Is a clean bill of health from the doctor,
And the kids shouldn't move back
 home for
  more than a year,
And not being audited, overdrawn, in
 Wilkes-Barre,
  in a lawsuit or in traction.

Happiness
Is falling asleep without Valium,
And having two breasts to put in my
 brassiere,

And not (yet) needing to get my blood
   pressure lowered,
      my eyelids raised or a second
         opinion.


And on Saturday nights
When my husband and I have rented
Something with Fred Astaire for the
   VCR,
And we're sitting around in our robes
   discussing
The state of the world, back exercises,
   our Keoghs,
And whether to fix the transmission or
   buy a new car,
And we're eating a pint of rum-raisin
   ice cream
      on the grounds that
Tomorrow we're starting a diet of fish,
   fruit and grain,
And my dad's in Miami dating a very
   nice widow,
And no one we love is in serious trouble
   or pain,

And our bringing-up-baby days are far
    behind us,
But our senior-citizen days have not
    begun,
It's not what I called happiness
When I was twenty-one,
But it's turning out to be
What happiness is.

# STILL FIFTY

# BY MY AGE

By my age I thought I would finally be
    able to
Finish *Moby Dick*,
Wait for the meal to be served without
    eating the roll,
And display unruffled composure when
    I'm at a cocktail party
        where I don't know a single soul
And nobody talks to me,
Instead of wanting to run and hide in
    the bathroom.

By my age I thought I would finally be
    able to
Read a tax return,
Admit that I'm wrong when I'm
    wrong — and not gloat
        when I'm right,

And display serene acceptance when I
    watch my married son
        walk out into the cold and snowy
            night
In a pair of torn sneakers
Instead of screaming, Stop! You'll
    catch pneumonia.

By my age I thought I would finally be
    able to
Speak coherent French,
Refrain from providing advice unless
    someone begs,
And display mature detachment when
    this lady M.B.A. with
        perfect skin and even better legs
Makes a play for my husband,
Instead of plotting to push her face in
    the pasta.

By my age I thought I would finally be
    able to
Cope with Celsius,
Drive to New Jersey without getting
    lost every time,

And display a mature and serene and
   composed and detached
      and unruffled acceptance of all
         that I'm
Still not able to do
By my age.

# SECOND MARRIAGE

He is a recent widower, very eligible.
She is a recent widow, attractive and
 bright.
And after several wonderful evenings
 together, they
  have decided that they are
Right for each other.

So as soon as their CPAs have
 reworked their tax structure,
And their doctors have pronounced
 them physically fit,
And their lawyers have found a formula
 for an equitable
  pre-nuptial agreement,
They intend to get married.

And he'll sell his condo in Aspen
　　because she hates skiing.
And she'll sell her house at the beach
　　because he hates sand.
And they'll merge their books and their
　　records and their
　　　　paintings and their furniture and
Their families:

His son who, at thirty, is having a
　　spiritual crisis.
Her son who, at thirty, still hasn't
　　started to date.
His daughter, who is deciding between
　　becoming a single parent
　　　　and going to business school.
Her daughter, who wants to know if
　　they are planning, when they
　　　　die, to be buried next to their first
　　　　　　or their second mate.
His brother, who thinks he should have
　　picked somebody younger.
Her sister, who thinks his taste in
　　jackets is crude.
Her father, who has a lot to say about

why Ronald Reagan was one
of our greatest presidents.
Her mother, who has a lot to say about
fiber and digestion
and why a person should never eat
fried food.
His aunt, who only hopes he knows
what he's doing.
Her uncle, who is either having a major
nervous breakdown
or being followed by the CIA.
Her aunt, who talks about Charles and
Diana as if — though she
actually doesn't — she actually
knows them.
His uncle, who talks with his mouth
full because — he explains — if
he waits till he's done, he always
forgets what it is he intended
to say.
Her cousin, who wants to sell them
more life insurance.
His cousin, who wants to sell them
some tax-free bonds.

And as soon as their therapists help them feel just a
Little bit fonder of each other's families,
They intend to get married.

# BRIEF ENCOUNTER AT THE DELICATESSEN

# BRIEF ENCOUNTER AT THE DELICATESSEN

She has no muscle tone. He has no hair.
But when they meet beside the deli case,
Some force within their blood begins to
    race.
He orders half a pound of roast beef,
    rare,
Plus one pound of corned beef and of
    tongue,
Along with coleslaw and a rye with
    seeds.
(Do married middle-agers have no
    needs?)
(Is untamed passion only for the
    young?)
His heart beats fast. Her thoughts are
    most unclean.

But mad desire yields to law and will.
She buys three whitefish and six pickles,
  dill,
Plus half a pound of hot pastrami, lean.

Then silently they part as (sigh) they
  must,
Surrendering to brunch instead of lust.

# THEY'RE BACK

# THEY'RE BACK

When our last child left home we were
    terribly sad and dejected.
We were done with our parenting duties
    and felt disconnected.
We missed all the children, of course,
    but we fully expected
They would thrive in the world and
    live happily ever after.

When our last child left home we were
    terribly sad — for a minute.
But a whole new life beckoned, and we
    were prepared to begin it.
We planned for a glorious future with
    no children in it.
Let them thrive and do well and live
    happily ever after.

Our last child was gone for a month
 when we started receiving
Bad news from the eldest. Her marriage
 was through. She was leaving.
And soon she moved back to her room
 to do yoga and weaving,
And to blame us for not living happily
 ever after.

Then our middle son called us, collect,
 to announce he was
 yearning
To go back to school for another degree.
 He'd be earning
No money, and therefore was counting
 a lot on returning.
He's in his room studying happily ever
 after.

Our youngest got married and found
 that he couldn't afford her.
And so he reminded us how very much
 we adored her,
Then asked if we wouldn't be willing to
 bed and to board her.

They're both in his room loving happily
    ever after.

When our last child left home we felt
    sad, but we rapidly mended.
Now the children are back, and the
    future we started has ended.
The hot water runs out routinely. We
    hadn't intended
For six to be showering happily ever
    after.

Our children are home and too old to
    be told, Wear galoshes.
But too young, it seems, to wash dishes,
    for nobody washes,
Though they finish a week's worth of
    food in just one evening's noshes.
Yes, they're sitting around eating
    happily ever after.

Our children are home and we can't
    find the scissors or car keys.
There are sweat socks all over the living
    room. Whose the hell

are these?
Each night we gaze up at the sky and
we wish on a star: Please
Let them go somewhere else and live
happily ever after.

# CHRISTMAS PRESENTS FOR FIFTY YEARS AND OVER

# CHRISTMAS PRESENTS FOR FIFTY YEARS AND OVER

He used to buy her lacy negligees.
She used to buy him jaunty turtlenecks.
But now they've moved into another
    phase:
More osteoporosis and less sex.

More Perrier, less Gevrey-Chambertin.
No sleeping — unawakened — through
    the night.
No cigarettes. No eggs. No beef. No tan.
And no, without bifocals, unblurred
    sight.

When Christmas comes, as it's about to
    come,

On what then do they plan to spend
  their dimes?
He's bought a pillbox for her calcium.
She's ordered him the large-type *New
  York Times*.

AND NOW YOU WANT
TO KNOW IF THERE
IS ANYTHING GOOD
TO SAY ABOUT
GETTING OLDER

# AND NOW YOU WANT TO KNOW IF THERE IS ANYTHING GOOD TO SAY ABOUT GETTING OLDER

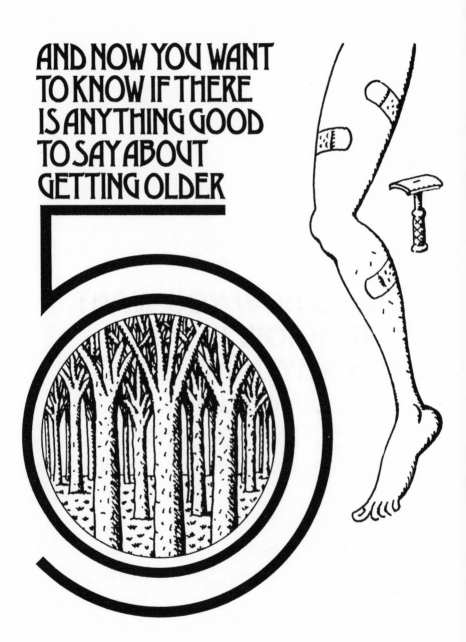

We aren't as self-centered as we used to
  be.
We're not as self-pitying — or as just
  plain dumb.
Middle age has come, and we find
(Along with the inability to sleep all
  night without
    a trip to the bathroom)
A few compensations.

We aren't as uncertain as we used to be.
We've learned to tell the real from the
  tinsel and fluff.
Getting old is tough, but we find
(Along with the inability to shave our
  legs unless
    we're wearing our glasses)
A few compensations.

We aren't as compliant as we used to
    be.
We choose our own oughts and musts
    and got-to's and shoulds.
We're deep into the woods, yet we find
(Along with the inability to eat a
    pepperoni pizza at
        bedtime)
A few compensations.

We aren't as judgmental as we used to
    be.
We're quicker to laugh, and not as eager
    to blame.
There's time left in this game. May we
    find
(Along with the inability to tell
    ourselves that
        we'll keep playing forever)
A few compensations.

# EIGHT BASIC FACTS
# ABOUT MEMORY

# EIGHT BASIC FACTS ABOUT MEMORY

The fact that people don't stop you
    when you ask them to stop
        you if you've told them this story
Doesn't mean that you haven't told it
    before.

The fact that you're only buying a
    couple of items at the store
Doesn't mean that you don't need to
    bring a list to the store.

The fact that you've put the passports in
    such a safe place that
        they couldn't possibly get lost
Doesn't mean that you actually,
    currently know where they are.

The fact that you've parked your car
   carefully
Doesn't mean, when the movie is over,
   that you will still recall
      where you parked the car.

The fact that you rushed upstairs
   because there was something you
      desperately needed in your closet
Doesn't mean, once you get there, that
   you'll recollect why
      you came.

The fact that you've known a person
   for thirty-five years
Doesn't mean, when you go to
   introduce him, that you can count on
      remembering his name.

The fact that you said good-bye and
   walked out the door
Doesn't mean that you won't be back
   immediately in order to get
      all the things you left behind.

And the fact that . . .
And the fact that . . .
And the fact that, the fact that, the fact
   that . . .

It's slipped my mind.

# HOW CAN PEOPLE WANT TO BRING CHILDREN INTO THIS TERRIBLE WORLD?

## (A POSSIBLE REPLY TO A POSSIBLE DAUGHTER-IN-LAW)

Everything good that once used to be
   wood is now plastic.
Whoever's in charge is either a crook or
   a creep.
And instead of from real human beings
We now get our money from money
   machines
And talk to each other after the sound
   of the beep.

But I still want a grandchild.

Going to lawyers can now cost us more
   than a Lear jet.

Going to bed can now give us a fatal
    disease.
A nuclear war, we've been told,
Will produce a nuclear winter so cold
That if we escape being roasted we're
    going to freeze.

But I still want a grandchild.

Terrorists blow us to pieces on foreign
    vacations.
Muggers and rapists attack us right on
    our own street.
And we're not even safe from harm
Locked up in our house with the
    burglar alarm
What with lead in our water and
    carcinogens in our meat.

But I still want a grandchild.

We've survived the decline and fall of
    the Roman Empire,
Endured Inquisitions, the Crash and
    the Second World War,

And lived through the Flood and the
  Plague.
So why don't you fertilize that egg
While I work on improving this planet
  a little bit more,

For my forthcoming grandchild.

# FOREVER FIFTY

# BEFORE I GO

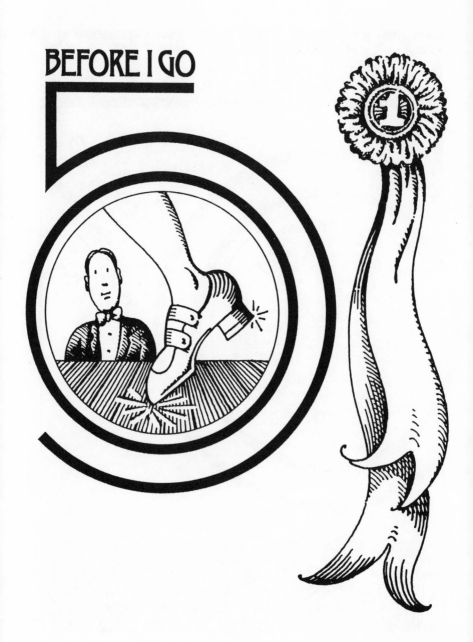

Before I go, I'd like to have high
   cheekbones.
I'd like to talk less like New Jersey, and
   more like
      Claire Bloom.
And whenever I enter a room, I'd like
   an orchestra
      to burst into my theme song.
I'd like to have a theme song before I
   go.

Before I go, I'd like to learn to tap
   dance.
I'd like to play seven-card stud like a
   pro, not
      a dunce.

And I'd like Robert Redford, just once,
  to slide his
      fingers down my back from my
        neck to my waistline.
I'd like to have a waistline before I go.

Before I go, I'd like to win the door
  prize.
I'd like to be thought of as valiant and
  brilliant and
      thin.
And I'd like, when offered a choice
  between duty and sin,
      to not immediately choose duty.
I'd like a couple of offers before I go.

Before I go, I'd like to make things
  better.
I'd like to be told I've been more of a
  joy than a pain.
And I'd like those I love to know that
  they are the ones,
      if I could do it again, I'd do it with.
I'd like to do it again before I go.

# YOU MIGHT
# AS WELL LAUGH

# YOU MIGHT AS WELL LAUGH

So your ex-husband's much-younger
   wife is having a baby.
So your stockbroker says your best
   stock is down 42 points.
So your mother has broken her hip and
   your cute little grandson
       has just switched from Oreo
          cookies to joints,
And you need a new hot-water heater,
   and roof, immediately.

It's important to gaze without flinching
   at life's cruel afflictions.
It's important to let yourself grieve, but
   please don't overdo.

Remember that, given a choice
    between laughter and slashing your
      wrists with a razor,
You might as well laugh.

So you got a D-minus on your last
    physical checkup.
So the claims court has finished
    deciding your case, and you lose.
So your dog ran away and your cute
    little granddaughter just
      switched from pigtails to dyeing
      her hair chartreuse,
And your auto insurance has
    doubled — effective immediately.

It's useful to face the harsh facts and
    decline self-deception.
It's no good denying the truth, but do
    try to eschew
Dark thoughts. For given a choice
    between laughter and throwing
      yourself off a building,
You might as well laugh.

So you've disappointed your parents
    and failed all your children.
So nobody's tried to seduce you since
    '76.
So your hair's falling out, and your cute
    little father has just
        switched from Chaplin revivals to
            porno flicks,
And your orthodontist recommends
    braces — immediately.

It's mature to endure the full pain. But
    avoid thoughts of nooses.
And continue the trip in your
    ever-more-leaky canoe.
For given a choice between laughter
    and pistols or pills or
        carbon monoxide,
Or dumping a large dose of arsenic in
    your stew,
You might as well laugh.

# SOME ADVICE FROM A MOTHER TO HER MARRIED SON

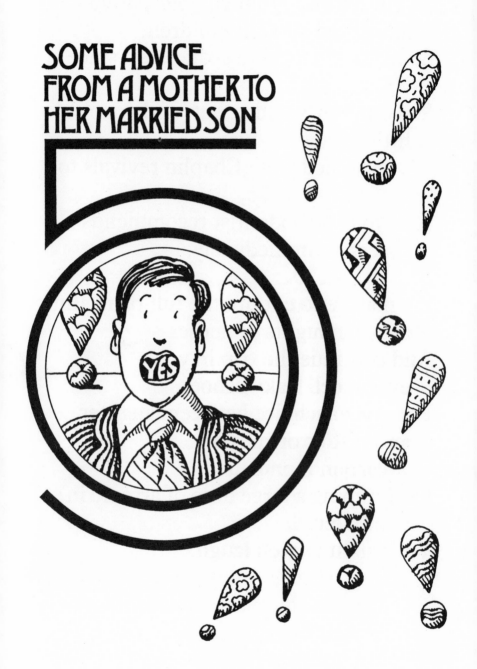

The answer to do you love me isn't, I
   married you, didn't I?
Or, Can't we discuss this after the
   ballgame is through?
It isn't, Well that all depends on what
   you mean by "love."
Or even, Come to bed and I'll prove
   that I do.
The answer isn't, How can I talk about
   love when the
      bacon is burned and the house is
         an absolute mess
      and the children are screaming
         their heads off and
      I'm going to miss my bus?

The answer is yes.
The answer is yes.
The answer is yes.

WHEN ASKED TO WHAT
THEY OWE THE SUCCESS
OF THEIR MARRIAGE,
HE AND SHE COMPLETELY
AGREE THAT LOVE IS
ACCOMMODATION

WHEN ASKED TO WHAT
THEY OWE THE SUCCESS
OF THEIR MARRIAGE,
HE AND SHE COMPLETELY
AGREE THAT LOVE IS
ACCOMMODATION

By six p.m. he's fainting from
    starvation.
She never thinks of food till nine at
    night.
They make a seven-thirty reservation —
He famished; she without an appetite.

He talks of cash flow and depreciation.
She talks of what is Beautiful and True.
And each endures the other's
    conversation
By gently nodding off until it's through.

They've different views of household
    decoration.
He loathes what she (and she what he)
    prefers.

But fair is fair. Their place of habitation
Holds tweedy armchairs (his), gilt
    cherubs (hers).

He wants to camp in forests on vacation.
She wants first-class hotels in Biarritz.
They therefore choose some
    compromise location
Midway between posh suites and
    snake-bite kits.

In bed they let no crazy wild sensation
Intrude upon their strict equality.
Instead, they work at joint gratification,
And work, and work, and work,
    relentlessly.

And comes their golden wedding
    celebration,
They'll praise each other for a job well
    done,
Agreeing, still, that love's
    accommodation,
But wishing that it could have been
    more fun.

# MEDICAL TESTS

# MEDICAL TESTS

My periodontist thought that Ezio Pinza
  was a battle in
    southern Italy.
My gastroenterologist couldn't tell
  Brian Donlevy from
    Brian Aherne.
My dermatologist didn't know to whom
  I was referring when
    I referred to Patti, Maxine and
      LaVerne.

My cardiologist thought that Little
  Sheba was a belly dancer
    from Cairo.
My orthopedist was unaware that
  Allyson, Havoc and Haver were
    three different Junes.
My urologist, when asked to hum the
  theme songs from "Let's

Pretend" and "Our Gal Sunday,"
    wasn't familiar with either
    the shows or the tunes.

My gynecologist thought that Gloria
    DeHaven was a retirement
        community.
My physiotherapist couldn't tell Victor
    Mature from Victor
        McLaglen or Vic Damone.
My ophthalmologist simply assumed
    that I was repeating myself
        when I alluded to Simone Simon.

My endodontist thought that a Porfirio
    Rubirosa was a skin
        rash.
My allergist, when pressed, could still
    not give the first and
        last name of Jack Benny's wife.
My internist was incapable of singing
    "Mairzy Doats." It has
        suddenly dawned on me
That I've put a bunch of kids in charge
    of my life.

# MORE
# QUESTIONS

# MORE
# QUESTIONS

Face lift, or no face lift — that is the
    question.
But I would like to mention fourteen
    others:
Are French-fried onion rings worth
    indigestion?
And why (although we vowed that we
    would never let this happen)
        have all us daughters turned into
        our mothers?
Will we, someday, grow unconcerned
    with fashion?
Is stoicism nicer than complaining?
Can reminiscence substitute for passion?
And how, now that we've saved our
    money for a rainy day,

do we determine if — in fact —
    it's raining?
Is dyeing an improvement over
    graying?
Is marriage an impossible profession?
Is the inevitable worth delaying?
And when (although we know
    confession benefits the soul)
        is silence even better than
            confession?
Can someone really have too much
    insurance?
Should we expect our children to be
    grateful?
When is quitting wiser than endurance?
And when did we decide "mature"
    meant settling for a spoonful
        when what we all still crave is the
            whole plateful?

# A SEXY
# OLD LADY

# A SEXY
# OLD LADY

I'm intending to grow up to be a sexy
  old lady,
With a gleam in my eye and lace on my
  underpants.
Never vulgar, of course, but a perfumed
  and pedicured lady
Whose passions persist long long after
  the age of romance.

I'm intending to walk around town as a
  sexy old lady,
The kind that no Boy Scout need hurry
  to help cross the street.
With a light-hearted bounce that
  announces now here comes
    a lady

Who knows all the steps to the dance
  and has not lost the beat.

I'm intending to finish my days as a sexy
  old lady.
Yes, spiritual too — and compassionate,
  wise, mature, droll.
But along with that high-minded stuff I
  shall still be a lady
Aware of the joys that lie just slightly
  south of the soul.

I'm intending to go to my grave as a
  sexy old lady.
There'll be plenty of time for propriety
  after I'm dead.
So if heaven has answered my prayers,
I expect to be found, around eighty,
  upstairs
With my sexy old husband nestled
  beside me in bed.

# THE PLEASURES OF
# AN ORDINARY LIFE

# THE PLEASURES OF AN ORDINARY LIFE

I've had my share of necessary losses,
Of dreams I know no longer can come
    true.
I'm done now with the whys and the
    becauses.
It's time to make things good, not just
    make do.
It's time to stop complaining and pursue
The pleasures of an ordinary life.

I used to rail against my compromises.
I yearned for the wild music, the swift
    race.
But happiness arrived in new disguises:
Sun lighting a child's hair. A friend's
    embrace.

Slow dancing in a safe and quiet place.
The pleasures of an ordinary life.

I'll have no trumpets, triumphs, trails
    of glory.
It seems the woman I've turned out to
    be
Is not the heroine of some grand story.
But I have learned to find the poetry
In what my hands can touch, my eyes
    can see.
The pleasures of an ordinary life.

Young fantasies of magic and of
    mystery
Are over. But they really can't compete
With all we've built together: A long
    history.
Connections that help render us
    complete.
Ties that hold and heal us. And the
    sweet,
Sweet pleasures of an ordinary life.

THORNDIKE-MAGNA hopes you have enjoyed this Large Print book. All our Large Print titles are designed for easy reading, and all our books are made to last. Other Thorndike Press or Magna Print books are available at your library, through selected bookstores, or directly from the publishers. For more information about current and upcoming titles, please call or mail your name and address to:

THORNDIKE PRESS
P.O. Box 159
Thorndike, Maine 04986
(800) 223-6121
(207) 948-2962 (in Maine and Canada call collect)

or in the United Kingdom:

MAGNA PRINT BOOKS
Long Preston, Near Skipton
North Yorkshire,
England BD23 4ND
(07294) 225

There is no obligation, of course.